Assessing Comprehension Thinking Strategies

by Ellin Keene

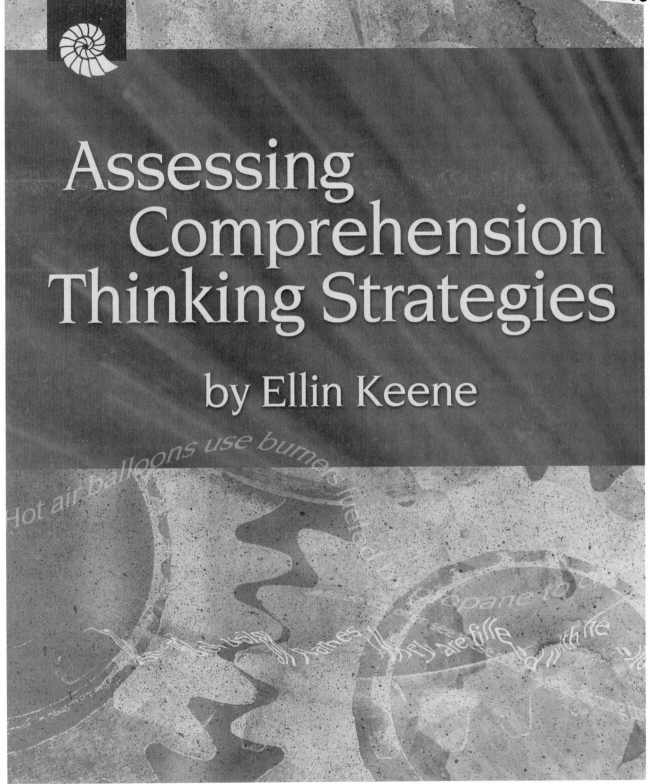

SHELL EDUCATION

Credits

Editor
Christine Dugan, M.A.Ed.

Editorial Manager
Gisela Lee, M.A.

Assistant Editor
Christina Hill

Production Manager
Peter Pulido

Project Manager
Lori Kamola, M.S.Ed.

Creative Design
Lee Aucoin

Editor-in-Chief
Sharon Coan, M.S.Ed.

Cover Design
Lee Aucoin

Contributing Author
Lori Kamola M.S.Ed.

Imaging
iserve Graphics

Publisher
Corinne Burton, M.A.Ed.

Shell Education
5301 Oceanus Drive
Huntington Beach, CA 92649-1030
http://www.shelleducation.com
ISBN 978-1-4258-0436-7
©2006 Shell Educational
Reprinted, 2008
Made in U.S.A.

Table of Contents

Foreword

by Ellin Keene

I can almost predict what the teacher's question will be when I see her hand go up at the end of my workshop. I can see the quizzical look on her face while she glances back over the notes to see if I've addressed her query so far. When she states the question, it usually comes out something like, "I completely agree that we ought to spend more time teaching kids how to comprehend, and I understand that the comprehension strategies are part of that instruction. I'm just not sure how to assess comprehension." Or, it might sound like, "My district has just written new report cards, and I have a hard time seeing how I can report a student's progress in comprehension using them." Sometimes, a teacher will ask, "We've been talking all day about teaching kids to think. But, how do you assess thinking? It's pretty tough to get in their heads, isn't it?"

Indeed, it is pretty tough to get in our students' heads, but that is exactly what comprehension assessment is all about. Short of taking them to the local medical center for an MRI, how do you "get into their heads" to know whether students are advancing their comprehension and thinking skills? This is exactly the dilemma many teachers face when they make fundamental changes in their approach to teaching reading comprehension—that is, when they begin to emphasize thinking throughout their curriculum.

I wish that we could all take the time to listen for hours as children talk about their insights and reactions to the books they read and the concepts they're struggling to understand. I've been trying (but only for 25 years!) to refine my own ability to truly "hear" a student's thinking based on what he or she says. I've found that, with very few exceptions, there is something meaningful in everything that a student shares, no matter how disconnected it may seem. There is something he or she is trying to communicate in those words, something that gives us insight into the depth of his or her understanding. If only we had the time to listen as much as we would like.

My colleagues at the Public Education & Business Coalition (PEBC) in Denver and I faced the same dilemmas when we began to explore the research in reading comprehension, particularly research which suggests that students' use of comprehension strategies deepens understanding in a wide variety of texts (Pearson, Roehler, Dole, & Duffy, 1992). How does one determine if they are using those strategies in order to comprehend more effectively?

We searched for assessments that addressed the use of comprehension strategies and found nothing. Individualized reading inventories that essentially ask students to recall, retell, and answer comprehension questions were not addressing our needs. I wanted a tool that actually

Foreword (cont.)

tapped into kids' thinking during reading, not before or after, and I wanted an assessment that asked kids to report on their thinking at a much deeper level than simply retelling or answering questions. Nothing was out there, so we designed one ourselves. Sometimes, particularly in education, you just have to invent the wheel yourself! The *Comprehension Thinking Assessment* is the result. It was first published as an appendix in *Mosaic of Thought* as the *Major Point Interview for Readers*, but it has been revised several times and is published here in several updated forms.

The *Comprehension Thinking Assessment* assesses students' thinking about a text by asking them to pause during reading to think aloud. I've found that this approach provides a much more accurate picture of student comprehension. When students learn to articulate their thinking about a text, either in oral or written form, they are able to go far beyond simply reporting on a particular text; they are reporting on their *thinking* about that text. That allows us not only to tell if they're "getting it," but also how deeply they are thinking about it—a far more sophisticated task.

My hope is that the *Comprehension Thinking Assessment* is, first and foremost, a flexible assessment tool. It is meant to be useful for classroom teachers who have anything but time on their hands. It can be used as a pre-/post-assessment on all the strategies, or it can be used before and after instruction on a particular comprehension strategy. The instrument is designed to be broken apart, providing a strategy-by-strategy assessment that can be administered (and scored) quickly, even in the context of a one-on-one conference with a child. For students who are more skilled at articulating their thinking in writing, the written form can be administered simultaneously to the entire class and scored later. The "Thinking Aloud" portions give teachers a general idea about how students comprehend a particular piece of text without asking them to retell and answer comprehension questions which are, in my view, less than valid ways to assess understanding. The rubrics can be used to chart progress—each point of growth (1–5) represents a 20% increase of points over the previous score. If you are assessing students with the same text level from pre- to post-assessment it is possible to talk about a 20%, 40%, or even 60 % growth over the pre-test. Those numbers can be communicated to parents or translated into grades for a report card.

It is important to remember that the *Comprehension Thinking Assessment* is just one tool among many that teachers can use in order to better understand their students' comprehension. I have found that I can learn every bit as much through conferring—listening intently and regularly—with students. Conferring is one of our most potent teaching tactics, and one that is indispensable when it comes to assessing a child's understanding. Conferring also

Foreword (cont.)

promotes new learning and encourages students to reach even deeper levels of understanding. Even the best assessment instruments cannot reveal what a student truly understands as he or she reads. In order to gain accurate insights into a student's thinking, we must engage in conversation with him or her.

Finally, I'd like to emphasize that my goal is not merely to have students use reading comprehension strategies. Rather, I hope that your students can learn to use comprehension strategies to better understand the texts they read and the concepts they encounter in all content areas. I'm always delighted to hear students talk about connections they make between the texts and their lives, but I must remember that using the strategies does not necessarily mean they comprehend more deeply. We need to go the next step to teach (and later, to assess) how using those strategies helps them comprehend more deeply or more effectively. This tool is designed to help teachers find out if kids, in fact, understand better than they did without using a comprehension strategy. However, teachers not only have to teach comprehension strategies, but also have to discuss *how* that strategy works to deepen comprehension. If our students can say, "I made a text-to-text connection *and* here's how it helped me better understand the character's emotions in this book," that is true comprehension.

Introduction

The assessments and rubrics in this book, developed by Ellin Keene with significant help from Anne Goudvis, co-author of *Strategies that Work* and with input from teachers and other staff developers, comprise an extensive reading comprehension assessment tool that examines how students think when they read. Teachers finally have a way to document a student's thinking process and score it, using procedures and methods that monitor growth in understanding.

How to Use This Book

Teachers can use the assessments in this book in a variety of ways. The "Thinking Aloud" assessment should always be given before using any of the other assessments, as it was designed to be an introduction to the others. Teachers may choose one of the options below to use the assessments in this book:

➡ Working with students one-on-one and having students read silently and complete each strategy assessment orally or in writing

➡ Working with students one-on-one and having students listen to or read aloud the text and then responding orally or in writing

➡ Working with students one-on-one and giving each strategy assessment as a pre- or post-strategy study assessment

➡ Working with small or large groups and having students complete a written assessment for all strategies using the provided leveled text or self-selected text

➡ Working with small or large groups and having students complete a written assessment as for one strategy as a pre- or post-strategy study assessment

➡ Working with small groups of students, reading a high-level text aloud to them, and having students complete a written assessment

Depending on the age of the student, administering the complete assessment takes between 20–45 minutes. Of course, choosing to use just one or a few strategies will take less time. The above scenarios can be divided into two categories of assessment—to inform instruction (formative assessment or screening assessment) or to assess learning (summative assessment).

How to Use This Book (cont.)

The first step is for a teacher to decide why he or she wants to assess student thinking. Once the purpose for assessment is determined, explore how to assess students. Keep in mind that the assessments in this book focus more on how students think about texts rather than how they retell or summarize a text.

To use this book to inform instruction: (What thinking strategies do students need to know?)

1. Decide which strategies you would like to assess. You may also complete the entire assessment (either in oral or written form).

2. Score the assessment using the rubric provided.

3. Design instruction based on the results of the assessment. For example, create small groups to focus more intensively on a given strategy, such as inferring.

Or, to use this book to assess learning: (What thinking strategies do students know well?)

1. Give the assessment as a pre-assessment.

2. Teach a unit of study on a strategy.

3. Give a second assessment as a post-assessment.

For a list of reading comprehension products and programs that focus on the strategies assessed in this book, see page 84. Here you will also find a list of books on the topic of reading comprehension recommended by the author.

Strategies Assessed in This Book

➡ Thinking Aloud

Readers need to monitor their own thinking while reading. Ultimately, they should be able to clearly articulate their thinking orally and in writing.

➡ Using Schema

Readers use schema (prior knowledge) purposefully to understand more thoroughly what they read. Prior knowledge includes information and experiences that contribute to and enhance what a reader already knows.

➡ Inferring

Readers infer by using both background knowledge and information learned from the text to draw conclusions, interpret, form opinions, and predict.

➡ Asking Questions

Readers purposefully generate questions before, during, and after reading to comprehend more completely what they are reading.

➡ Determining Importance in Text

Readers decide on the most important elements and themes in text content at the word, sentence, and whole-text level. A summary is a short and concise description of the main ideas in a text. A summary includes the key ideas and the main points that are most important for a student to note and remember.

Strategies Assessed in This Book (cont.)

➡ Setting a Purpose for Reading

Readers set purposes in order to make reading more meaningful. When readers understand the purpose for reading a particular text, they can select the appropriate reading strategies that help meet the reading goal.

➡ Monitoring Comprehension

Readers know when they are not comprehending, know what they need to understand, and have options for improving comprehension when a reading problem is encountered.

➡ Visualizing (Using Sensory and Emotional Images)

Readers create detailed images that contribute to comprehension. They can use these images to draw conclusions, make inferences, fill in missing information, and recall important details.

➡ Synthesizing (and Retelling)

Readers keep track of the meaning of text and their interpretations during reading and pull together information from a variety of sources after they read. They identify the underlying meaning of a text and extend their comprehension beyond the basic elements of a passage including forming opinions and reading critically. Retelling is describing what happened in a story or text after hearing it read or reading it.

➡ Text Structure/Structural Patterns

Authors structure texts in different ways to easily convey information to readers as they read. The elements of fiction story structure, or the "skeleton" of the story, are characters, plot, and setting. Readers understand the structure of a text in order to analyze how stories are organized and gain greater meaning.

What's Included in This Book

Passages

This book includes four reading passages for each grade level—two fiction and two nonfiction selections. The passages are coded with a letter to represent each grade. A = first grade, B = second grade, C = third grade, D = fourth grade, E = fifth grade, F = sixth grade, G = seventh grade, and H = eighth grade. Teachers may choose to use these passages as a beginning-of-year and end-of-year assessment, or they may use them as necessary throughout the year. This assessment does not measure the accuracy or fluency of a student's reading; instead, it assesses how well a student uses reading comprehension strategies to think about text. Teachers may also choose to use other grade-level appropriate passages from an Informal Reading Inventory's (IRI) additional assessment sources contained in the district's reading program, or other grade-level appropriate texts that students are currently reading. The first section of the book contains the reading passages which have been leveled using Flesch-Kincaid. These passages may be reproduced for classroom use.

Assessments: Oral and Written

All of the assessments in this book can be given either in oral or written form. Choose the assessment format that best suits the students. To administer the assessment as a listening comprehension tool or as an interview where the student reads the passage and the teacher asks the questions, choose the first assessment of each strategy, titled "Oral Assessment." To administer the assessment in written form, choose the second assessment of each strategy, titled "Written Assessment." The assessments in this book may be reproduced for classroom use.

Oral Assessment

The oral assessment form is designed for one-on-one assessment of a student using a text from a leveled passage included in this book. The teacher can read the passage, making it a listening comprehension assessment, or the student can read the passage aloud and the teacher can ask the questions and record the student's responses. If you prefer, use an IRI or other text the student is reading at the time of the assessment. This form may be most useful with young students, students who are learning English as their second language, and/or students who are not yet able to fully articulate their thinking in writing. After conducting a unit of study on a strategy, a post-assessment should be given using this same form, but with a different text that is at the same reading level as the pre-assessment. Post-assessment passages are also included in this book.

What's Included in This Book *(cont.)*

Written Assessment

Use the written assessment form to administer an assessment to a whole class or to a small group of students who are able to write responses to the questions after they are read aloud. Administer the assessment in two or three 30-minute blocks. If you are assessing only one or two strategies, give them at the same time. Use the grade-level appropriate text provided in this book (choose fiction or nonfiction) or use a graded passage from an IRI or other text that the student is currently reading. After conducting a unit of study on a strategy, a post-assessment should be administered in the same manner but using a different text at the same reading grade level. Post-assessment passages are also included in this book.

Rubrics

The rubric provided for each assessment is used for oral and written forms of assessment and follows the oral and written assessment for each strategy. The rubrics may be reproduced for classroom use. Use the rubric to record a student's scores on each set of questions. Circle the number corresponding to the statement that best reflects the student's response.

Some points to remember:

√ If using all the assessments with a student, you will repeat the "Thinking Aloud" assessment before assessing the "Determining Importance in Text" strategy to refresh the student's memory about the passage.

√ Consider all of the questions when assigning one score for each strategy.

√ When students go beyond explaining their thinking and begin to articulate how using a strategy increases comprehension, the response should be scored at least a "four."

CD-ROM

All of the reading passages, assessments, and rubrics in this book are included on the CD-ROM located on the back inside cover of the book. You may alter and print them for classroom use.

Correlation to Standards (cont.)

The No Child Left Behind (NCLB) legislation mandates that all states adopt academic standards that identify the skills students will learn in kindergarten through grade 12. While many states had already adopted academic standards prior to NCLB, the legislation set requirements to ensure the standards were detailed and comprehensive.

Standards are designed to focus instruction and guide adoption of curricula. Standards are statements that describe the criteria necessary for students to meet specific academic goals. They define the knowledge, skills, and content students should acquire at each level. Standards are also used to develop standardized tests to evaluate students' academic progress.

In many states today, teachers are required to demonstrate how their lessons meet state standards. State standards are used in the development of all of our products, so educators can be assured that they meet the academic requirements of each state.

How to Find Your State Correlations

Shell Education Publishing (SEP) is committed to producing educational materials that are research and standards based. In this effort, all products are correlated to the academic standards of all 50 states, the District of Columbia, and the Department of Defense Dependent Schools. A correlation report customized for your state can be printed directly from the following website: **http://www.shelleducation.com**. If you require assistance in printing correlation reports, please contact Customer Service at 1-877-777-3450.

McREL Compendium

SEP uses the Mid-continent Research for Education and Learning (McREL) Compendium to create standards correlations. Each year, McREL analyzes state standards and revises the compendium. By following this procedure, McREL is able to produce a general compilation of national standards.

Each reading comprehension strategy assessed in this book is based on one or more McREL content standards. The chart on the following page shows the McREL standards that correlate to each reading comprehension strategy and the assessments used in the book. To see a state-specific correlation, visit the SEP website at **http://www.shelleducation.com**.

Correlation to Standards (cont.)

Objective	Comprehension Strategy	Pages
Uses strategies to convey a clear main point when speaking (e.g., expresses ideas in a logical manner, uses specific vocabulary to establish tone and present information)	Thinking Aloud	52–54
Reflects on what has been learned after reading and formulates ideas, opinions, and personal responses to texts	Thinking Aloud	52–54
Makes connections between characters or simple events in a literary work or nonfiction text, and people or events in his or her own life	Using Schema	55–57
Uses prior knowledge and experience to understand and respond to new information	Using Schema	55–57
Makes, confirms, and revises simple predictions about what will be found in a text (e.g., uses prior knowledge and ideas presented in text)	Inferring	58–60
Makes, confirms, and revises simple predictions about what will be found in a text (e.g., uses prior knowledge and ideas presented in text, illustrations, titles, topic sentences, keywords, and foreshadowing clues)	Inferring	58–60
Generates questions about topics of personal interest	Asking Questions	61–63
Asks questions to obtain information, seek elaboration, and clarification of ideas as well as to seek other's opinions and comments	Asking Questions	61–63
Previews text (e.g., skims material, uses pictures, textual clues, and text format)	Determining Importance	64–66
Summarizes and paraphrases information in texts (e.g., includes the main idea and significant supporting details of a reading selection)	Determining Importance	64–66

Correlation to Standards

Objective	Comprehension Strategy	Pages
Establishes a purpose for reading (e.g., for information, for pleasure, to understand a specific viewpoint)	Setting a Purpose for Reading	67–69
Establishes and adjusts purposes for reading (e.g., to understand, interpret, enjoy, solve problems, predict outcomes, answer a specific question, form an opinion, skim for facts; to discover models for own writing)	Setting a Purpose for Reading	67–69
Uses specific strategies to clear up confusing parts of a text (e.g., pauses, rereads the text, consults another source, represents abstract information as mental pictures, draws upon background knowledge, asks for help, questions whether the text makes sense)	Monitoring Comprehension	70–72
Uses meaning clues (e.g., picture captions, title, cover, headings, story structure, story topic) to aid comprehension and make predictions about content (e.g., action, events, character's behavior)	Monitoring Comprehension	70–72
Uses mental images based on pictures and print to aid in comprehension of text	Visualizing	73–75
Uses new information to adjust and extend personal knowledge base	Synthesizing and Retelling	76–79
Uses text organizers (e.g., headings, topic and summary sentences, graphic features, typeface, chapter titles) to determine the main ideas and to locate information in a text	Text Structure/ Structural Patterns	80–82
Understands structural patterns or organization in informational texts (e.g., chronological, logical, or sequential order; compare-and-contrast; cause-and-effect; proposition and support)	Text Structure/ Structural Patterns	80–82
Knows setting, main characters, main events, theme, sequence, and problems in stories or texts	Text Structure/ Structural Patterns	80–82

The Research

Comprehension Matters

"The message is clear—the most important thing about reading is comprehension" (Block, Gambrell, & Pressley, 2002). Real comprehension is more than just retelling and answering questions about the story. Meaningful comprehension involves thinking, learning, and expanding a reader's knowledge (Keene & Zimmerman, 1997). Students are taught how to use comprehension strategies effectively so that they can learn to use these strategies independently to increase understanding of what they read. Knowing just one technique can improve comprehension, but knowing multiple strategies helps students become truly solid readers who can understand many kinds of texts (Duke & Pearson, 2002).

Comprehension instruction should be balanced—it needs to provide both explicit instruction (i.e., thinking aloud, modeling, etc.) in comprehension strategies and a great deal of time spent reading, writing, and discussing text (Duke & Pearson, 2002). Students need to read and understand a variety of texts; it is important to provide many opportunities for reading and to practice comprehension strategies daily.

Strategic Reading

Strategic reading involves a reader's conscious application of specific cognitive strategies (Honig, Diamond, Gutlohn, & Mahler, 2000). Teachers need to show students how to use these strategies so they can monitor and enhance their own comprehension, becoming increasingly independent in their use of strategies over time (Duke & Pearson, 2002). Reading comprehension is a complex process involving interaction between the reader and the text, requiring the reader to use multiple skills. This process begins before a student starts to read, when he or she activates background knowledge and sets a purpose for reading. A teacher can provide the purpose, or the student can create his or her own purpose for reading. Strategic reading occurs when the reader tests prior knowledge with new information, questions, infers, and creates mental images.

The reader brings background knowledge, or schema, to the text. Students need a variety of background knowledge and experience to be successful readers. They need to understand the way words are printed on the page, the purpose of printed material, and the relationship between printed and spoken language. Personal experience or knowledge about the topic is also helpful. If such knowledge is lacking, the teacher should provide necessary background information and help students revise such knowledge as they continue through a text.

The Research (cont.)

Understanding Text Structures

There are features of a text that affect comprehension. Sometimes readers find complicated sentences difficult to understand; they need to think about the context of the text to aid in discovering its meaning. Information within a text can be arranged in various ways; students must understand that arrangement and how it contributes to the meaning of the selection. Two examples of text organized in specific ways to produce meaning are chronologically ordered paragraphs, and cause-and-effect paragraphs. Students can be taught to recognize these various features of the text through systematic instruction and repeated exposure to a wide variety of reading material. When students understand why and how a text is arranged in a particular way, they gain an enhanced understanding of the material they are reading.

Activities to Enhance Comprehension

Pre-reading, during-reading, and post-reading strategies can increase comprehension. Some pre-reading strategies include purpose questions, predicting, previews, anticipation guides, semantic mapping, writing before reading, and creative drama. Pre-reading strategies can activate prior knowledge and give students a purpose for reading. These activities motivate students to want to read and understand the text. During-reading strategies promote comprehension as a student reads, and they include guided questions, cloze procedure, and metacognitive strategies. Post-reading activities help students expand on the learning gained from the text and combine new information with prior knowledge. Post-reading strategies include questions, visual representations, reader's theater, retelling, and applications. Some strategies—like discussions, semantic webbing, mapping, and writing activities—can be used at more than one stage of the reading process.

Types of Readers

It is critical for students to think and be aware of their thinking as they read. When students develop an awareness of their thinking process, they can consciously choose to use strategies that will aid their comprehension. Readers can be categorized into four main types of thinking while reading (Perkins & Swartz, 1992, as cited in Harvey & Goudvis, 2000).

The Research (cont.)

1. The first type of reader lacks an awareness of his or her thinking process when reading.

2. The second type of reader realizes when the comprehension process breaks down, but does not have sufficient strategies to use to overcome the problem of lack of comprehension.

3. The third type of reader uses thinking and comprehension strategies to improve understanding and learn new information. This reader can monitor and solve problems encountered while reading.

4. The fourth type of reader is highly strategic about thinking and comprehension. This reader is flexible, is able to select a variety of strategies to use for better comprehension, and is aware of the specific goals and purposes for reading.

Comprehension is an interactive process involving many factors, including the reader's background information, the information from the text, the interaction of the reader's schema with the text, the reading situation, and the purpose for reading. Students need to be taught how to increase their comprehension using various reading and thinking strategies; they need to be guided through this process with teacher modeling and support. When all of these factors work together, students achieve higher levels of comprehension when reading.

Why Assessment Is Important

Assessment is an integral part of good instruction and should be conducted regularly. "Assessment is the collection of data, such as test scores and informal records, to measure student achievement, and evaluation is the interpretation and analysis of this data. Evaluating student progress is important because it enables the teacher to discover each student's strengths and weaknesses, to plan instruction accordingly, to communicate student progress to parents, and to evaluate the effectiveness of teaching strategies" (Burns, Roe, & Ross, 1999). Many different types of assessment tools are available for teachers, including, but not limited to: standardized tests, reading records, anecdotal records, informal reading inventories, portfolios, diagnostic assessments, and formative and summative assessments. These different types of assessments serve different purposes, but few are truly effective at measuring and documenting comprehension in reading. In this book, the assessment tools provided can be used as both formative/screening assessments and summative assessments for understanding reading comprehension strategies. Teachers use formative assessment to help them make good decisions about the kind of instruction their students need (Honig et al.,2000).

The Research (cont.)

Formative assessment is usually an ongoing process. Summative assessment shows teachers what students have (or have not) learned from their instruction. This type of assessment shows growth over time and also helps to determine what to teach next or what needs to be re-taught.

When students comprehend what they are reading, they are learning new information and creating meaning in the text or story. A growing body of evidence reveals the importance of knowing what students are thinking as they read and finding out the reasons that they are able to understand and connect with their reading. Stephanie Harvey and Anne Goudvis (2000) state, "The only way we can confidently assess our students' comprehension is when they share their thinking with us." It is important to keep track of students' thinking about reading and, more importantly, students need to know about their thinking as well so they can work to improve comprehension. The assessments in this book both stimulate students to think about their comprehension skills and reading strategies, and show the teacher what needs to be taught or what has been learned. Comprehension is complex. Simple checklists often are not enough to show what students really understand; making notes (or having students write their thoughts) about students' thinking provides a deeper understanding (Cunningham & Allington, 2003).

The Loose Tooth

Thomas has a loose tooth. Thomas uses his tongue to wiggle the loose tooth. The tooth does not fall out.

Thomas uses his finger to wiggle the loose tooth. The tooth still does not fall out.

Thomas is sad. He is sad because the loose tooth will not fall out. Mom gives Thomas a big, shiny, fat, red apple. Thomas takes a big, big, bite. Out comes Thomas's loose tooth. Only it is not loose anymore. Now it is lost! He smiles, and there is a big gap where his tooth used to be—out at last!

Down by the Pond

Anna and Jeffrey took a walk by the pond. They saw an egg in the mud. The egg was big and white. They could see that the egg was cracking.

"Look!" said Anna. "There is an egg, and it is cracking!"

"I see it too," said Jeffrey. "What kind of egg is it?"

"I don't know," said Anna.

Anna and Jeffrey stood and watched the egg. Soon they saw a leg come out.

"Look!" said Anna. "I see a leg!"

Soon they saw a head come out of the egg.

"Look!" said Jeffrey. "I see the head!"

When the baby came out of the egg, Anna and Jeffrey saw it was a baby turtle. The baby turtle looked just like its mom and dad. It had a shell just like them. The shell was hard and green. It had a head, four legs, and a little tail, exactly like its mom and dad!

"Look!" said Anna. "It's a baby turtle!"

"I see the baby turtle too," said Jeffrey.

The baby turtle slowly left the egg and walked to the water. The baby turtle dove into the water and swam away. Anna and Jeffrey couldn't believe what they just saw! They couldn't wait to share it with their friends.

Bird Talk

Birds live all over the world. Birds are the only animals with feathers. Some birds have colorful feathers and some birds have dull feathers.

All birds have two legs. Some birds can walk on their legs, and some birds hop on their legs. Some birds can stand on one leg!

All birds have wings. Some birds can fly with their wings. Some birds cannot fly with their wings, but they sure look pretty!

All birds have beaks. They can use their beaks to pick up food. Some birds can use their beaks to open nuts or seeds, and some birds can use their beaks to go fishing! Birds can also use their beaks to carry things.

All birds lay eggs. Birds use sticks, rocks, or string to make a nest. The birds lay their eggs in the nest. The mom or dad bird sits on the eggs to keep them warm.

The smallest bird is the hummingbird. The largest bird is the ostrich. Which bird do you think lays the bigger egg?

Helpful Bugs

Do you like bugs? Some people are scared of bugs. Some people think bugs are creepy! But some bugs are very helpful.

Ladybugs are helpful bugs. Ladybugs are red and black. They can also be orange and black. Ladybugs eat aphids. Aphids are bad bugs. Aphids eat the leaves and stems on plants. This is not good. When ladybugs eat aphids, they help keep plants looking nice.

Bees are other helpful bugs. Bees are yellow and black. Bees can be big. Bees can be small. Bees sip nectar from plants. Bees make honey from the nectar. This is helpful because people like honey for food. But watch out! Bees can sting!

Do you know any other bugs that are helpful?

The Special Gift

It was a very special day for Ben. It was his favorite day of the year. Today Ben was turning eight years old. He had invited ten friends to share the fun with him, and they would arrive soon.

But Ben was not smiling, and there was a stain on his shorts from a fallen tear. He looked outside. The balloons he had tied to the mailbox were starting to get wet.

Ben thought of the games he wanted to play in the backyard. His dad had found sacks for three-legged races. "Now," Ben whispered, "that's ruined."

A car drove into the driveway. His friend Danny jumped out and yelled, "Happy birthday!" He handed Ben a present. Another car arrived. Ben's mother announced, "Oh, look. It's Alex. And look, Ben," she continued, "another very special guest has come out for your party."

Ben turned his head and looked at the sky. He covered his eyes from the bright light. He felt the heat on his face. The guest he had been waiting and hoping for had come to his party. "It's going to be a great party after all!" Ben yelled.

To the Zoo

It was field trip day. Miss Ray was taking her class to the zoo. She got to school early to get the name tags ready.

In the morning the children came into the room. Miss Ray handed out the name tags. "Everyone choose a partner," she said. "Then we'll get on the bus!"

The children got on the bus and sat in a seat with their partners. Parents joined the class to help. The bus was noisy! They sang songs and talked about the animals they hoped they would see.

When the bus arrived at the zoo, Miss Ray said, "We will all stay together and follow the path to see the animals."

After they saw many different animals, Miss Ray said, "It's time to go back to school!" The class climbed back on the bus. This time, there were not many sounds on the bus, except the sounds of snoring!

Art Museums

An art museum is a fun place to be. You can see all kinds of art. Go see the paintings on display. Some are big and some are small. Some are all one color and some show many colors. There are so many exciting ways to paint. No two paintings are ever the same. Artists make each artwork an original piece.

Go see the sculptures. There are some sculptures made of clay. There are other sculptures made of wood. Sculptures can be made from anything, even metal or objects you find on the ground. You can walk all the way around a sculpture.

I like to look at sculptures from the back.

Some art museums have a corner just for kids. You can learn about art history in these places. Sometimes you can create an artwork of your own. Be sure to practice at home to improve your skills. Maybe your art will be in a museum one day.

At the Library

Have you been to a library lately? A library has all the books you need. It has books that tell your favorite stories. It has books on any topic you can name. It does not cost money to borrow a book. All you need is a library card. You can get a card at the front desk. The card will have your name on it.

Libraries today have more than just books. Some have movies. Some have music. You can borrow movies or music with your card, too.

Most libraries have a place just for kids. This is the best part of the library. Everything you want is in one place. You can ask for help. A librarian knows where everything belongs. Librarians can help you find what you need.

So find your local library and see the books today!

The Dream

Yesterday in school during math class, John sat at his desk and yawned. Then he couldn't stop yawning. Then his friend Penny started yawning. Before long, Rob and Sue were yawning, too.

Even Mrs. Hunter let out a big yawn as she wrote some math problems on the chalkboard.

John looked around the room and everyone was yawning!

Now everyone's eyes were closing. Mrs. Hunter's eyes kept opening and closing, too. John heard Sue snore, then he heard Rob snore and Penny was snoring, too. John could not believe it. Everyone was falling asleep and snoring.

John listened to the snores and watched everyone sleeping in class. Then it happened. John let out a big yawn and his eyes popped open. He looked around the room. He wasn't in school at all. He was at his desk at home trying to work on some math problems and had fallen asleep in his chair. All that snoring and yawning had been a dream. What a relief!

Bucket by Bucket

Mom and Mike go to the beach on a sunny Saturday afternoon. Mike builds a sandcastle, while Mom reads a book on her beach towel.

First, Mike uses a shovel to fill a bucket with sand. He packs the sand tightly down in the bucket.

Next, he pours a little bit of water in the bucket. This gets the sand wet. Water helps keep the sand together.

Mike turns the bucket over onto a flat area of sand and lifts up the bucket. The sand stays together, and now Mike has started to build his castle.

Then Mike fills and empties the bucket again and again. Soon his castle has walls and towers. Finally, Mike digs holes for windows and doors.

He's almost done when waves come up and take his castle out to sea. Time to start over again!

Sliding Along

You lift a leaf in a shady, dirt-filled garden, and there it is. It's an animal that moves slowly on one big foot. What is it, you wonder? It's a snail!

Snails can live on land and in the water. All snails have a hard shell covering their bodies.

You can keep water snails in the water in a fish tank. They will help keep the glass clean.

Like most snails, a land snail has two feelers on its head. It also has eyes and a mouth on its head. Snails don't like hot and dry weather and stay in shady, moist areas. During very cold winter weather, snails hibernate in the ground.

Most land snails eat rotting plants. They also eat flowers, and many gardeners aren't happy when they see snails.

Everywhere it goes, a land snail leaves a trail of slime that it pours out as it moves. The slime helps the snail move on its one foot. The foot is a big body part, made mostly of muscle. This muscle moves in a wave, taking the snail with it. When a snail is disturbed, it pulls itself into its shell to stay safe. Also, if the weather is too dry, the snail can retreat into its shell and seal off the entrance to protect its body from drying up.

If you see a one-footed animal letting out slime, it's most likely a snail.

Play the Piano

A piano is a musical instrument that has 36 black keys and 52 white keys. Each key is hooked to a small felt hammer. To play a piano, you press down a key. When a key is pressed down, its hammer hits the string, and the string vibrates, making a sound.

Some keys hit short strings, which make a high sound. Other keys hit long strings, which make a low sound.

The keys for the lowest sounds are on the far left of the piano. The keys for the highest sounds are on the far right. Many keys can be played at the same time. If you play certain keys together, you're making music!

You can learn to play the piano after you learn to read music. When you can read music, you can see how the notes are supposed to be played to make songs sound a certain way. Playing the piano takes work, but it can be fun, too.

Best Friends

Alessandra and Sarah are in fourth grade. They are best friends. They spend all of their time together in class, after school, and on the weekends, too. The girls have been friends for two whole years. They never fought, not until that day.

"Alessandra, can I borrow your new pencil?" Sarah asked. Alessandra's dad had just given her a special pink pencil with hearts on it, and it had a heart-shaped eraser.

"Of course, Sarah, you're my best friend, right?" answered Alessandra.

Sarah used the pencil for the afternoon. As they were walking home, Alessandra asked for her special pencil back. Sarah looked, but she couldn't find it! She checked her backpack, her pocket, and behind her ear.

Alessandra was so upset that she ran home and cried. She was mad at Sarah for being so careless. She wondered if her dad would be mad, too.

The next day at school Sarah and Alessandra ignored each other. They had never gone a whole day without speaking! When Alessandra got home, her dad noticed the big frown on her face and the tears in her eyes.

Alessandra told him what happened. Her dad said that he wasn't mad and she shouldn't be either! Sometimes accidents happen, even between best friends.

Alessandra realized she had been silly. She called Sarah and said she was sorry for getting mad. Sarah said she was sorry for losing the pencil in the first place. They made up and decided never to get mad at each other again.

The Spelling Bee

The final round of the Jefferson School Spelling Bee is tomorrow, and Jonas, Manuel, and Kyla are the final three contestants. They were all winners in their class spelling bees, and now they must compete against each other for the school spelling bee.

Jonas isn't looking forward to the spelling bee. He doesn't like spelling bees that much and doesn't think they mean anything. He doesn't care if he wins or not. So Jonas decides to play football all afternoon rather than study. That night he plays video games on the Internet, too!

Manuel wants to win very badly. He thinks spelling bees are important and can prove who is the best speller. He studies the words all night long. He has his mother quiz him several times, using flash cards and a timer. He even practices spelling the words backwards! Manuel wants to be prepared.

Kyla has never been in a contest before. She feels nervous and sick to her stomach. She wants to win, but she is not sure she can. She tries to study, but the words are hard to spell. She gets frustrated, so she gives up and goes to bed.

At 9:00 the next morning, the spelling bee begins. The contestants each stand in front of their class numbers. As the whole school watches, Mr. Phelps reads the words one by one. After several rounds, there is a winner. The class claps and cheers for the winner. "Congratulations!" said Mr. Phelps. "Now, it's on to the City Championship! And if you win there, you'll go to the State Championship!"

What Makes an Insect an Insect?

How are a bee, an ant, and a fly the same? For one thing, they are all insects. They all have six legs and three main body parts, called the head, the thorax, and the abdomen.

An insect's head has eyes and a mouth, and many have antennae, too. Insects use their antennae to feel, taste, and smell things.

The middle part of an insect's body is called the thorax. If an insect has wings, this is where they are located.

The hind part of an insect's body is the abdomen. It is usually the largest part of an insect's body. People have abdomens too, but some people might call their abdomen a belly.

Insects have skeletons, too. But their skeletons are on the outside of their bodies, and they are called exoskeletons. The skeletons are very hard, so they protect the soft inside part of the insect's body.

So the next time you see a bug, look at it closely. Is it an insect or not? How can you tell?

George Washington

George Washington was America's first president. He was important. Washington was born on February 22, 1732. He lived in Virginia. He had five brothers and sisters.

In school, math was George's best subject. He stopped going to school at age 15. This was not unusual at the time.

George had many jobs when he was young. He was a soldier. He worked as a farmer. He had other jobs, too.

In 1759, he married his wife, Martha. She had been married before. She had two children. George and Martha did not have children of their own.

George took a new job in 1775. He led Americans in the Revolutionary War. They won the war. America became its own country.

In 1789, George was elected president of the United States. He was 57 years old. George was president for eight years.

When George died, the capitol of the United States was moved near his home. It is called Washington, D.C., and is named after George!

Have you seen his face on a U.S. dollar bill?

The Treasure Hunt

The neighborhood treasure hunt was about to start. Everyone was at the starting point and had his or her instructions. Ming and her family were fifth in line in their car, behind their other neighbors. The loud and shrill whistle sounded, and the cars took off.

Ming quickly looked at the list and decided it wasn't that long. First on the list was a basket full of flowers. They drove around the neighborhood looking everywhere. When they turned the last corner, Ming spotted a magenta basket of almost-dead flowers at the end of someone's driveway, which meant they got 50 points!

The next item on the list was a stray shoe. They headed through back roads and alleys toward the grocery store. Her father pointed out a tennis shoe that was lying on the road by a dumpster. Ming was excited; they now had 50 more points!

Now for the third item on the list—a discarded barbecue grill. That wasn't too hard—it was the end of the barbecue season. They soon had 50 more points when they saw an old, rusty grill in a vacant lot.

There are two more items to go—an electric sign with burned-out bulbs on a store and a red convertible. They found the sporty red convertible when they passed the car dealership. Fifty points for Ming's family! One more to go and only 15 minutes in which to find it and get back to the starting point. Ming's dad smiled at her as he turned the car around and headed toward home. Ming was worried and wondered why he was heading home. Then she remembered that two blocks from their house was an electronics repair shop. She saw it and noticed that the "o" on the sign was dark. Ming shouted, "Score!" Everything on the list was accounted for, so the family headed to the finish line. It had been a great day of family fun with the neighborhood treasure hunt!

The Dilemma

Sophia Washington was the new girl in class. Her family had just moved to town from out of state, and she didn't know anyone, not even her neighbors! She was scared to death to go to her new school, but her parents said she had to go anyway. Sophia had always been on the shy side, and making new friends was hard for her.

She walked into the classroom with her stomach in knots. Her palms were sweaty too, because she was so nervous. As she stood in front of the room being introduced by the teacher, a girl in the third row caught Sophia's eye. They smiled at each other, and Sophia relaxed a little bit. Maybe it wouldn't be so bad after all. She was happy when the teacher sat her right next to the girl who had smiled at her. Kari introduced herself to Sophia and offered to show her around school and introduce her to some other people in class.

The two girls ate lunch together all week and talked on the phone all of the time after school. Sophia was glad that Kari was her new friend. Kari even asked her to go shopping with her and her older sister, Samantha. Sophia hoped her parents would say yes and let her go.

On Saturday, the three girls went to the mall to hang out, go shopping, and have lunch. They were standing at a jewelry counter looking at all of the sparkly bracelets, when Sophia noticed that Samantha had picked up something shiny. As Sophia watched, Samantha quickly looked around and put the shiny object in her pocket. Sophia couldn't believe her eyes! What was she supposed to do now? Kari was her only new friend at school, but how could she be friends with her when her older sister was shoplifting? Should she tell Kari? Should she tell Kari's parents or her own parents? If Samantha got caught, would Sophia get in trouble too? She didn't know what to do; this was the worst dilemma she had ever had to deal with. Sophia wished her parents had never moved to this new town in the first place.

Animal Talk

Humans communicate with each other all the time. We talk, phone, write, email, and text message.

Animals can't do these things, so how do they communicate with each other?

We've all heard dogs bark and growl, and cats meow and purr. Making sounds is the most common form of animal "talk." Dogs make sounds when they're scared, happy, or angry, and they make sounds to warn you. Gorillas and beavers make throaty sounds. Some animals, like grasshoppers, make sounds by rubbing their legs together.

Some animal talking is done through marking. Special markings on an animal may tell another animal its species, age, or sex. A scratch on a tree made by an animal is another type of marking.

Honeybees dance to show where a new source of food is. Certain female animals send out smells that attract males. And we all know how skunks tell us that they're threatened!

Other animals use touch to talk. Wolves wrestle to figure out their rank in the pack. There are even animals that light up to talk! Eels and lightning bugs are two examples.

One way humans are like animals is when we communicate without using our voices, like using sign language or body language. Humans can learn so much just by watching each other. So maybe we don't have to be Dr. Doolittle after all. Maybe we already know what the animals are saying.

Will the Real Tasmanian Devil Please Stand Up?

Have you heard of a Tasmanian devil? Does the name make you think of a cartoon? Do you know that there really is such a thing as a Tasmanian devil? It comes from Tasmania, in Australia.

The Tasmanian devil is an animal about the size of a large dog. It can grow to be about 30 inches, or 0.8 meters, long. It can weigh up to 22 pounds, or 10 kilograms. A female is smaller than a male. Some people say a Tasmanian devil looks like a bear because it has dark fur, its jaws are large, and its teeth are strong.

Its name comes from the devilish look on its face. It has a hoarse snarl and a bad temper. You might think it would be a good hunter, but the Tasmanian devil is actually quite lazy. Rather than hunt for food itself, it lets others hunt. It eats their scraps — bones, fur, and all.

Tasmanian devils sleep during the day, which means they're nocturnal, or awake at night. They're easy to hear at night because they are noisy eaters.

At one time, Tasmanian devils were almost extinct. They were killed off by dingoes, or wild dogs, from Australia. They are now a protected species, so their numbers are increasing again.

The Litterbusters

Elizabeth was riding the public bus downtown with her older brother, Brian. It was pretty hot outside, so they decided to get off the bus and buy some cold drinks. They got their refreshments and took a walk down the street toward the museum.

As they waited at the crosswalk, they saw a fancy, expensive-looking new car pull up. As they admired the car, the passenger door opened a bit and out rolled an empty juice bottle. Then the light turned green and the car sped off.

Elizabeth and Brian could hardly believe it. Who would deliberately throw trash in the middle of the street? Brian noticed all the other garbage in gutters and on the sidewalks. He explained to Elizabeth how much he hated litter and how lazy it was to be a "litterbug." They decided that they had to get their neighborhood cleaned up because it looked horrible.

When they got home, Elizabeth and Brian wrote a letter to the mayor of their city.

They suggested that the city put public trash cans on every corner, and described how they felt about people littering in their town. They wrote that they wanted to see the streets and sidewalks cleaned up. They even had everyone in the neighborhood sign the letter to give it more impact. Then Brian mailed it to the mayor.

A few weeks later, Brian told Elizabeth he wanted to show her something. He took his sister for a walk up the street. What do you think they saw? There were new trash cans on every corner and hardly any litter on the sidewalks!

The mayor had listened to them. Elizabeth and Brian were happy and proud. They decided they would always help keep their town clean.

Maria Rosita and the Mukluk Song

Hundreds of years ago, in a kingdom far away, there lived a girl named Maria Rosita. She lived with her poor father at the foot of a great mountain. Maria Rosita always sang lovely songs to keep her father happy. However, she had to be careful not to be heard by anyone but her father, for the Giant Mukluk was bound to come if he heard. The Giant Mukluk was a creature of the mountain who wanted to steal all music and make the world a gloomy place.

One day, Maria Rosita was singing her tune softly and pulling a cart of coal to their hovel when, suddenly, she heard a great banging and clanging. She was sure it was the Giant Mukluk and that he had heard her song. Bravely, she sang louder and louder to show him she was not afraid. After many minutes passed, the clanging stopped.

This went on for many days. Maria Rosita hummed her song and did her chores. The banging would come and Maria Rosita would sing her lovely song louder until the noise stopped.

One day, there was no banging or clanging. As Maria Rosita hummed softly, she saw a pretty lavender butterfly outside the window. She sang her tune to the butterfly until it fluttered away.

The following day, the lavender butterfly came again. This time, it brought with it a handsome prince! The prince explained that he had been the Giant Mukluk. He had come to steal her music, but when she kept singing louder, her singing soothed him. Her brave and beautiful song broke the spell that made him so gloomy!

Maria Rosita and her father went to live in the prince's castle. There she sang her lovely songs all day and made every heart glad.

Elephant and Woolly Mammoth: Are They the Same?

The woolly mammoth roamed Earth from about two million years ago until 9,000 years ago. Elephants are related to mammoths, and are similar in many ways.

The biggest difference between the elephant and mammoth is hair. Mammoths lived during the last ice age and needed thick fur to help keep them warm. The African elephant lives in hot, dry places and the Asian elephant lives in warm, moist areas. Because elephants don't have to worry about keeping warm, they don't need the same furry coat.

Mammoths had long trunks that were not quite as long as the African elephant's trunk. They were more like the size of the Asian elephant's trunk, perhaps just a bit longer. Like elephants, mammoths were herbivores. That means they didn't eat meat. Just as you may have seen elephants do, mammoths used their trunks to drink and to grab food. They could eat up to 600 pounds (273 kilograms) of food every day!

Both male and female mammoths had huge, curved tusks. Male and female African elephants also have long tusks. Female Asian elephants don't have any tusks at all.

Mammoths had large ears, but they were not as big as those of elephants now. The African elephant has huge ears, which helps get rid of body heat, keeping the elephant cooler. As you can see, elephants and mammoths are a lot alike, but they are not the same!

The Great Pyramids

The pyramids of Egypt are said to be some of the most amazing buildings on Earth. A pyramid is defined as a large building with a square base that has four sloping, triangular sides. The sides come to a point at the top. The pyramids of Egypt were made of enormous blocks of stone. These stones were laid so perfectly that not even a tiny space was left between them. A pyramid took thousands of workers and many years to complete.

Egyptians used the great pyramids as tombs for pharaohs, or kings. The most famous pyramids were built about 4,500 years ago. Egyptians thought a person lived forever, and that when a person died in one life, he or she went on to the next life. They mummified, or dried and preserved, the kings' bodies and buried them in these great tombs. They put treasures and food in the tombs for use in the next life.

Many large pyramids were surrounded by smaller ones, which were used for the king's wife and children. The king's officials were also buried nearby in small tombs. These tombs, called mastabas, had sloping sides and flat roofs.

The ruins of 35 major pyramids and 40 small ones still stand near the Nile River. The largest is the Great Pyramid of Khufu. It was 481 feet, or 146 meters, tall when built and it was Earth's tallest building for more than 4,000 years!

These huge buildings provide clues to ancient times. They also serve as a reminder of Egypt's great past.

At the Circus

It was an extra special day for Leticia because her family had three tickets to the circus. Leticia had never been to a circus, so she was very excited and couldn't wait to see what it was all about. She had often heard about the mysterious performers and incredible animals, but she didn't entirely know what to expect.

As they entered the large, striped tent called the Big Top, a funny-looking clown came up to Leticia and asked her to pull the lavender flower on his shirt. When she did, water squirted out of the flower onto the clown's face, which made Leticia laugh loudly. She shook the clown's hand and told him she appreciated his wacky sense of humor.

Leticia and her family found their seats just as a drum roll announced the beginning of the show. During the first act, three clowns entered the ring, which is a round area where the action takes place. The clowns used balls, bicycles, and hoops to perform many tricks. Their childish jokes made the entire audience laugh so loudly that Leticia's ears hurt from the noise, and her cheeks hurt from smiling.

Next, a man entered a different ring with two ferocious-looking tigers. Leticia was worried that the man would get hurt, but her uncle told her that the tigers were well trained. The trainer led the tigers around the wire cage several times. The trainer had the tigers sit on tall, narrow stools and jump through a fire-lit hoop! Leticia was still nervous and felt her heart beating fast, but she enjoyed the thrilling act.

After that, five elephants and two elephant trainers entered a third ring. Leticia was overjoyed to see her favorite animals. It was amazing to watch the huge elephants balance on top of tiny stools. A lady in a beautiful, sequined costume climbed up on top of one elephant and spread her arms out wide. Then the elephant began to walk on its two hind legs.

The last performers to come out and entertain the audience were a high-wire team. The team was a group of men and women who walked on wires high above the ground. The wires were only about as thick as Leticia's thumb! Some members of the team carried a pole for balance. Others strapped their legs onto ropes and hung upside down, twirling hoops around their arms at the same time. A few of the men and women did many dangerous flips and turns on swings. Leticia's aunt explained that these performers train for many years to learn these tricks.

When the final act was over, Leticia got up with her aunt and uncle to leave. The same clown that she had met when they arrived handed her a giant flower made from bright balloons. Leticia couldn't imagine a better way to spend the day, and she thanked her aunt and uncle profusely for the invitation to spend the day with them.

Small Girl in a Big Town

Tuesday was an extremely depressing day for Gloria because she was leaving her house, neighbors, friends, and school to move to a new home in the city.

"Do we really have to go, Mom?" asked Gloria sadly, through tears.

"Oh, Gloria! I'm sorry that you're so upset," replied Mom with a sigh. "But I think that you'll like living in a city. Life there will be much more exciting and interesting. You will be able to experience culture and diversity, and you will learn so much more about the world. Trust me, in time you will be grateful that we are providing you with this opportunity to expand your knowledge of the world."

Gloria didn't find Mom's words very comforting. Gloria had never moved before, and she didn't want to now. She had lived in a small town in a rural area her whole life, and she could not imagine living in a city and leaving behind all that she knew. The only thing on her mind was how nervous she was and how terrible it would be when she got to her new home!

As they approached the city, Gloria looked out of the window and noticed the beautiful skyline. She had never seen so many tall buildings before, and some of her initial fear was replaced by excitement.

"Look at those amazing buildings! I can't believe how tall they are and how many there are. Will we be living in one of them?" asked Gloria.

Mom and Dad nodded their heads yes, and a small smile spread across Gloria's face.

Dad drove the car down the busy streets as Gloria took in all the sights. She saw a video store, a pet shop, a grocery store, a library, restaurants, and a beauty salon. They stopped at several lights, and after making more than a few turns, finally arrived in front of their new home. And it was indeed an elegant skyscraper!

They parked the car in the underground garage and rode up the mirrored elevator to the twenty-fifth floor. The first thing Gloria did when she went inside was to look out the floor-to-ceiling window in the main living room. The view all around was absolutely amazing! She saw other tall buildings, the rooftops of shorter buildings, parks, and even the school she would attend. Gloria imagined that she could see her old home in the country.

Saying good-bye to her friends had been difficult and sad for Gloria, but she was looking forward to attending a new school and meeting new friends. She decided to have a good attitude and explore the unfamiliar city—it would be an adventure!

Gloria began to realize that even if you are unhappy or frightened, you can still try to make the best of things. Making life fun is all about keeping your attitude positive!

Earth's Largest Animals

Have you wondered what the largest animals on Earth are? The answer to that question depends on where you look—on land, or in the ocean. On land, the largest animals are African elephants. What could possibly be larger than an elephant, you might ask? Well, the blue whale is bigger! Not only is it the largest sea animal, it is even bigger than an African elephant!

While African elephants are the largest land animals on Earth, they are tiny in comparison to blue whales. African elephants can be about 3.5 meters, or 11.5 feet tall at the shoulder and can weigh almost 5.5 metric tons, or 6.6 tons. In comparison, blue whales can be about 30 meters, or 105 feet long and weigh about 135 metric tons, or 148.5 tons. That's a big difference! In fact, blue whales are the largest of all animals that have ever lived on Earth.

Both African elephants and blue whales are mammals, which means that the females of both animals produce milk to feed their babies. Mammals are also warm-blooded. The body temperature of elephants and whales remains about the same no matter where they are. All mammals are covered by hair at some point in their lives, although neither African elephants nor blue whales have very much hair. As adults, they both have just a few bristles here and there. Mammals also breathe air through lungs. While a whale must come to the surface of the water to breathe, blue whales usually stay near the surface of the water since that is also where their food is.

Both elephants and whales have a good sense of hearing—both can hear low-pitched sounds that humans cannot hear. Although whales have very good sight, they have no sense of smell. Elephants, on the other hand, have poor eyesight and a good sense of smell.

People have used both the blue whale and the African elephant as resources. For example, people have hunted the whale for food and oil. Elephants have been trained to do work and are prized for their ivory tusks. Today, agreements, or laws, protect these giant mammals so that they can continue to live in their natural habitat without facing extinction.

The Busy Life of Honeybees

Although there are about 20,000 kinds of bees in the world, honeybees are the most useful to people because they produce honey, which people use as food, and beeswax—a substance that is used to make candles, crayons, and makeup.

Honeybees are social bees that live in groups, called colonies, inside hives. A hive might be a special white, rectangular box or a hollow area in a tree. The central structure of the colony is the wax comb, which is made up of six-sided, white wax chambers, or rooms. Some honeybee colonies have as many as 80,000 members. There are usually three types of bees in a colony—a queen, workers, and drones—and each type has a specific role to perform.

The queen's only job is to lay eggs, and in the spring, the queen lays about 2,000 eggs a day! Each colony has only one queen, who may live for up to five years. If the old queen disappears or becomes feeble, a new queen is made. Sometimes a young queen fights with an old queen until one stings the other to death.

A drone's only job is to mate with the queen. There can be up to 500 drones in each colony. Drones aren't able to hunt for food because their tongues are too short to suck up nectar from flowers, so they depend on worker bees to feed them. Drones live in the hive in the summer, but in the winter, worker bees may kick them out of the hive if there isn't enough food.

Worker bees neither lay eggs nor mate because they have other jobs to do. They spend their entire lives performing duties, or jobs, and thousands of them live in a colony. At the beginning of their lives, workers clean the hive and feed other bees. Then they produce wax and build honeycomb cells. Later, they protect the hive and eventually hunt for food. Workers hunt for food by sucking up nectar from flowers with their long tongues. Back in the hive, workers put the nectar in an empty cell, where it changes into honey. A worker bee can live for anywhere from six weeks to several months.

People thousands of years ago ate honey that they stole from hives found in trees. Today, farmers keep hives of bees, usually in boxes, and sell the honey that the bees make. Beekeepers have learned to handle their bees carefully and take their work very seriously. They wear special clothing, including gloves for their hands and veils to protect their faces so they don't get stung. If you find a hive of bees on your property, you can call a beekeeper to come and collect your bees! Thanks to the amazing and busy lives of bees, we can enjoy the sweet and sugary taste of honey and the fresh clean scent of candles.

Theodore's Supermarket

Theodore had a big homework project assignment for the weekend. He was supposed to design his own ideal supermarket. The best way to do this, according to his teacher, was to go to the local supermarket and analyze how the store is arranged.

Since Sunday was shopping day for his dad, Theodore took his notebook and tagged along. Arriving at the supermarket, Theodore's dad grabbed a shopping cart. Theodore made a note for his supermarket plan: "Make sure carts aren't noisy," he wrote down immediately.

As they entered the store, Theodore noted the produce section. Apples, bananas, potatoes, sprouts, asparagus, and onions were bagged. Using the big, white scales, Theodore weighed each bag to see what it cost and placed it in the cart, thinking about each step in the process. Then he mapped out where he thought the scales would go in his store to be the most convenient for customers. Theodore's dad, the family chef, spun around a rack displaying little bags of spices and picked out taco seasoning for one of the dinner recipes that week.

The next aisle was brimming with food in cans and jars. Theodore updated his diagram to include black beans, refried beans, peas, sauces, salsas, and soups. Confounded by the dizzying shelves of soups, Theodore noted that the ones in his store would be better organized so people could find things easily.

Slowly, they went up and down every aisle in the store as Theodore's dad stocked up on their family staples. Theodore mapped out where certain departments would go and how his shelves would be arranged.

A sign read "Home Supplies" in the next aisle. Theodore imagined how he would organize these items while his dad picked out a few things they needed. Sponges, dish soap, laundry soap, brooms, mops, recycling bags—all these things were neatly organized.

The last part of their shopping trip was the dairy aisle. Theodore realized how well planned this was, so customers could choose their dairy products last and let them remain cold in the dairy case while they did the rest of the shopping. Theodore, figuring his dairy aisle should also be near the checkout area, mapped out his store. His dad picked up some milk, eggs, margarine, and sour cream. "We're out of orange juice, too," Theodore reminded him.

The shopping was finally done, and so was Theodore's map. Later on, having put the finishing touches on his store, Theodore wondered what other kinds of buildings he could design someday and thought that perhaps a career as an architect might be in his future.

The Messy Room

"Mom, where's my favorite baseball hat?" Nathaniel bellowed loudly down the hallway. Nathaniel couldn't find anything in that disordered and chaotic room of his.

Nathaniel's room was a disaster; actually, it was a complete catastrophe. Clothes overflowed from his laundry basket like a pot boiling over, smelling like old socks. Dirty, sticky dishes littered the room from left to right, and baseballs, footballs, and even basketballs, were tossed everywhere.

"You're worried about finding your hat? Take a second and explain where that floor of yours has disappeared to these days," his mom responded with a holler. She was exhausted from arguing with Nathaniel about his room; if he wanted to let it be such a disgusting mess, he had to live with the consequences.

As Nathaniel searched through his closet, camping equipment and a skateboard from the high shelves plummeted to the floor with a crash. His twin sister, Jacqueline, casually sauntered into the room and surveyed the mess.

"What are you looking for?" she asked, a devilish look in her eyes and a smirk on her face.

"My lucky baseball hat—the blue and orange one that Grandpa William gave me," Nathaniel answered, slightly panicked at this point.

Jacqueline sighed an exasperated sigh. She was sick of this misplaced disarray, too. Each day it was something new—perhaps a lost shoe or a missing book. It didn't matter. Nathaniel's belongings always went missing, and it usually happened at the most inopportune moments.

However, today Jacqueline decided to be sympathetic because she realized that being unkind wasn't going to remedy the problem—Nathaniel needed to learn his lesson. Jacqueline decided to take things into her own hands and have a little conversation with her parents.

Following baseball practice that day, Nathaniel came home to a completely different house. Dirty breakfast dishes were piled high in the sink while newspapers, magazines, and a week's worth of mail were all scattered on the countertops in complete disorder. In fact, Nathaniel could barely open the front door because there were numerous pairs of shoes heaped up in the foyer!

"What's wrong with this house?" Nathaniel exclaimed as his whole family walked into the kitchen with him.

"Nathaniel, we thought you liked things messy," said his dad.

"Well . . . ." Nathaniel pondered for a minute. Did his room really look this messy all of the time?

Nathaniel's family convinced him that cleanliness is happiness, and after that day Nathaniel learned his lesson and decided not to be such a slob!

Customs of the World

There are more than six billion people living on Earth right now, on various continents, in different countries, with different cultures and customs. Groups of people with similar beliefs and ways of living share a culture, and the way these groups interact with each other and conduct their lives are called customs. For example, a custom in Saudi Arabia and Iran is for women to be covered when they are in public places. In China, people say their last names first in order to honor their family names.

In each culture, there are behaviors or customs that are a regular part of life. For example, people from different cultures greet each other differently. The Japanese and the Chinese bow, while people in India clasp their own hands together, and some groups in Africa raise one arm when they meet others. Kissing the hand of a superior person is done in some cultures. French men and women kiss each other on both cheeks as a greeting, but people in the United States shake hands to greet each other. The idea of shaking someone's right hand dates back to ancient Greeks, who used it as a sign of friendship.

Knowing different customs is important, especially if you travel to other countries. For example, it is considered a sign of respect to stick out your tongue in Tibet, but that would be rude in other parts of the world. In Indonesia, it is not polite to point your feet at someone or touch someone's head. These actions are not considered rude in other places. People in India take off their shoes in a place of worship, and the Japanese don't wear shoes in homes or schools.

In the United States, people keep their shoes on in schools and places of worship. Women open the door for men in South Korea, but it is just the opposite in Europe. People in India hiss to get attention. Would this be considered proper in your culture? In Vietnam, it is rude to make eye contact with someone else. In other places it is acceptable and even expected, especially if someone is speaking to you.

It is important to know and respect the customs of people from all different cultures. People would appreciate each other more and have more understanding if they only took the time to learn the customs of others.

Terra-Cotta Soldiers Stand Guard

At the tomb of Qin Shi Huang, the first emperor of China, thousands of terra-cotta soldiers have been standing guard for the past 2,000 years. These sculpture warriors are an amazing sight and were first discovered in 1974.

In 1974, farmers were digging a well by the tomb in Xian, China, and unexpectedly found some pottery. Archaeologists came to dig in the area and found what they believe is an underground palace—a place for Emperor Shi Huang to spend eternity. It took about 720,000 workers at least 39 years to build the entire structure. So many treasures were buried with Shi Huang that the burial site needed to be guarded. Archaeologists think rivers of liquid mercury flowed in the tomb and that arrows were set as traps.

Although the actual tomb of the emperor has not been found, more than 8,000 life-size pottery soldiers have been uncovered. Only the legs of the soldiers are solid pottery, while their bodies, heads, and arms are hollow. Each soldier weighs about 250 pounds (114 kilos). The warriors do not all look the same—they have different ears, noses, and hairstyles. Some soldiers have beards, and some have mustaches. There are soldiers who look proud, mean, and angry, yet others are smiling. You will find soldiers that are standing and others that are kneeling.

The designs and colors of the clothing are different as well. Some warriors were sculptured wearing armor, which was most likely painted brown or black. The soldiers carried different weapons, such as metal spears, swords, or wooden weapons. The emperor wanted his grave to be guarded for all eternity by a replica, or model, of his own army as they stood guard. Over time, most of the color has faded from the uniforms worn by the terra-cotta warriors, which may have been originally painted bright red or green.

Other things were found at the site, too, including chariots and horses. The life-size chariots are made of bronze. The horses have large nostrils and big eyes. The terra-cotta animals look like they are waiting to go into battle. They are ready to protect their emperor—even in death!

Many people think that Emperor Shi Huang's tomb is the eighth wonder of the world.

Student's Name:_____ Date:_____

 # Thinking Aloud: Oral Assessment

Directions: Read aloud the following instructions to the student. Record the student's responses below each question/statement.

Teacher:

I want you to tell me as much as you can about the first few lines of this passage as you (or I) read it aloud. I am going to stop you during the reading so you can tell me what you are thinking as you read (or listen to me read).

Now, I want you to tell me exactly what you were thinking about. The important thing is that you pay attention and remember the story (or text), so that you can tell me what you were thinking about during the reading. You can tell me anything that the book makes you think about, any problems you had during the reading, and what you think it is about.

Note➡ Identify logical stopping places, roughly every third or fourth page in picture books, and every two to three paragraphs in longer text. Read and stop and repeat the above procedure when you have read enough text to allow the student to think aloud.

_____

_____

_____

_____

_____

_____

Thinking Aloud: Written Assessment

Directions:

Read silently for three minutes. When you are told to stop, write as much as you can remember about what you were thinking about as you read the passage. It is most important that you pay attention and remember the story (or text), so that you can write everything you were thinking about as you read. You can write anything the passage makes you think about, any problems you had while reading it, and what you think the passage is about.

Note➡ Repeat the directions for students until they finish the passage. Give them five minutes to write their initial thoughts about the text.

_____

_____

_____

_____

_____

_____

_____

_____

_____

Student's Name:_____ Date:_____

 # Thinking Aloud: Rubric

Use this rubric to record the student's scores on each set of questions. Circle the number corresponding to the statement that best reflects the student's response. If this is done with other assessments, consider both "Thinking Aloud" assessments when scoring the rubric.

1	No response, random thoughts unconnected to the text.
2	Disconnected thoughts relating more to the pictures than text.
3	Thinking is tied to text events/text content; may be inaccurate in relation to text, more tied to personal experience; may identify problems (word or text level) during reading; may include a rough retell.
4	Demonstrates two or three of the following skills: may generate questions; may identify conflict within the text; may infer; may discuss connections between text events and own experience; may make predictions about overall book meaning; may include a detailed retelling; may talk about how his/her thinking changed as he/she read or listened.
5	Clearly expresses own thinking; may speculate about theme, discusses how own thinking supports or inhibits comprehension.

Observation Notes:

_____

_____

_____

_____

Using Schema: Oral Assessment

Directions: Read the following instructions to the student. Record the student's responses below each question/statement.

Teacher:

I want to ask you some questions about what you think about while you (or I) read.

A. When you read (or listened) to the text, did it remind you of anything you know about or believe? What? Why did it remind you of that? (If student's response is no, ask, "Did it remind you of any experiences or things that have happened before?")

_____

_____

_____

B. Are there things you know about your life, yourself as a reader, this author, or this type of text that help you to understand this book? How does that help you to understand better?

_____

_____

_____

C. Choose one of the questions below to ask the student:
- We have just talked about what this book reminds you of. (Restate student's response.) What do you understand now that you did not understand before?
- How does schema or background knowledge help a reader understand a text while reading?
- How did thinking about your own schema or background knowledge help you understand this text?

_____

_____

_____

Student's Name:_____ Date:_____

 # Using Schema: Written Assessment

Directions: Answer some questions about what you think about while you read.
Use the space below each question to write your answer.

A. When you read that text, did it remind you of anything you know about or believe? What?
Why do you think you remembered what you did?

_____

_____

_____

B. Are there things you know about your life, yourself as a reader, this author, or this type of
text that help you to understand this book? How does that help?

_____

_____

_____

C. Choose one of the questions below to answer:
- You have just written about what this book reminds you of. What do you understand
now that you didn't understand before?
- How does schema or background knowledge help a reader understand a text while
reading?
- How did thinking about your own schema or background knowledge help you
understand this text?

_____

_____

_____

Student's Name:_____ Date:_____

 # Using Schema: Rubric

Directions:

Use this rubric to record the student's scores on each set of questions. Circle the number corresponding to the statement that best reflects the student's response. Consider all three questions when scoring the student.

1	No response/schematic connection.
2	Can talk about what text reminds him/her of but cannot explain; reference to schema may not be clearly connected to text.
3	Relates background knowledge/experience to text.
4	Expands interpretation of text using schema; may discuss schema related to author or text structure; may pose questions based on apparent discrepancies between text and background knowledge.
5	Explains how schema enriches interpretation of text; talks about use of schema to enhance interpretation and comprehension of other texts; connections extend beyond life experience and immediate text.

Observation Notes:

_____

_____

_____

_____

Student's Name:_____ Date:_____

 # Inferring: Oral Assessment

Directions: Read the following instructions to the student.
Record the student's responses below each question/statement.

    A.   Choose from narrative text or expository text for question A.

- For narrative text: **When you read (or heard me read) could you predict what was about to happen? Why did you make that prediction? Can you find something in the book that helped you to make that prediction? What do you already know that helped you make that prediction?**

- For expository text: **In addition to what you have read (or heard me read) so far, what do you think the author wants you to know or learn at this point in the text?**

_____

    B.   Select an event or fact from the text that calls for a conclusion, opinion, or interpretation. Refer to the event or fact when asking the following questions.

- **What did the author mean by _____? What details in the text help you to know that? What do you already know that helped you to decide that?**

_____

    C.   **What do you know about this text that the author didn't write?**

_____

    D.   Choose one of the questions below to ask the students:
- **We have just talked about inferring.** (Restate one of the child's conclusions, opinions, interpretations, or predictions and identify it as an inference.)
  What do you understand about this text now that you didn't understand before?

- **Why do readers understand better when they infer? Why should readers infer? How does inferring help a reader understand a text better?**

_____

Student's Name:_____ Date:_____

 # Inferring: Written Assessment

Directions: Answer some questions about what you think about while you read.
Use the space below each question to write your answer.

A. For narrative text: Can you predict what is about to happen? Why did you make that
prediction? Can you identify something in the book that helped you to make that
prediction? What do you already know that helped you to make that prediction?

_____

_____

_____

B. For expository text: In addition to what you have read so far, what do you think the author
wants you to know or learn at this point in the text?

_____

_____

C. What do you know about this text that the author didn't write?

_____

_____

D. Choose one of the questions below to answer:
• You have just written about your inferences. What do you understand about this text
now that you didn't understand before?

• Why do readers understand better when they infer? Why should readers infer?

• How does inferring help a reader understand a text better?

_____

_____

Student's Name:_____ Date:_____

 # Inferring: Rubric

Directions:

Use this rubric to record the student's scores on each set of questions. Circle the number corresponding to the statement that best reflects the student's response. Consider all three questions when scoring the student.

1	No response/inference.
2	Attempts a prediction or conclusion that is inaccurate or unsubstantiated with text information.
3	Draws conclusions or makes predictions that are consistent with text or schema.
4	Draws conclusions and/or makes predictions and can explain the source of the conclusion or prediction in text.
5	Develops predictions, interpretations, and/or conclusions about the text that include connections between the text and the reader's background knowledge, ideas, or beliefs that enhance the overall meaning of the text and make it more memorable to the reader. Discusses why/how inferences help him or her understand better.

Observation Notes:

_____

_____

_____

_____

Asking Questions: Oral Assessment

Directions: Read the following instructions to the student. Record the student's responses below each question/statement.

A. **What did you wonder about while you (or I) read this text?**

_____

_____

B. **What questions do you have now about what you (or I) read?**

_____

_____

C. Choose one of the questions below to ask the student:

- **We have just talked about the questions you asked during reading. (Restate student's response.) How do questions help you understand more of what you're reading?**

- **What do you do when you are reading and a question comes into your mind? Do questions help you understand some kinds of text better than others? Tell me more about that.**

_____

_____

Student's Name:_____ Date:_____

 # Asking Questions: Written Assessment

Directions: Answer some questions about what you think about while you read. Use the space below each question to write your answer.

    A.   What did you wonder about while you were reading this story/text?

_____

_____

_____

    B.   What questions do you have now about what you read?

_____

_____

_____

    C.   Choose one of the questions below to answer:

- You have just written about the questions you asked while you were reading. How do questions help you understand more of what you're reading?

- What do you do when you are reading and a question comes into your mind? Do questions help you understand some kinds of text better than other kinds?

_____

_____

_____

Student's Name:_____ Date:_____

 # Asking Questions: Rubric

Directions:

Use this rubric to record the student's scores on each set of questions. Circle the number corresponding to the statement that best reflects the student's response. Consider all three questions when scoring the student.

1	No questions and/or poses irrelevant questions.
2	Poses literal question(s) that relate to the text.
3	Poses questions to clarify meaning.
4	Poses questions to enhance meaning of text (critical response, big idea); may explain how posing questions deepens comprehension.
5	Uses questions to challenge the validity of text or author's stance/motive or point of view and to enhance his/her understanding of the text; questions may be rhetorical and lead to interesting discussion. Can explain how asking questions enhances understanding.

Observation Notes:

_____

_____

_____

_____

Determining Importance in Text: Oral Assessment

Directions: Read the following instructions to the student. Record the student's responses below each question/statement.

A. Are there some parts of this text that are more important than the others? Which ones? Why do you think they are the most important?

_____

_____

B. What do you think the author thinks is the most important part so far in the text? What signals or clues did the author use to make you believe _____ (restate student's response) **was important?**

_____

_____

C. Choose one of the following:

- **We have just talked about parts of the text** (restate student's response) **that you feel are important. How does thinking about the more important parts help you to understand the text better?**

- **Do you think or do anything while you are reading that helps you remember the important parts?**

- **Do you ever have trouble remembering what is important after you read? How do you solve that problem?**

_____

_____

Note➡ If assessing all of the comprehension strategies, repeat the "Thinking Aloud" Assessment (page 52) with a continuation of the text that the student is reading. Then, continue with the remaining assessments. If assessing only the "Determining Importance in Text" strategy, you do not need to reassess the "Thinking Aloud" process at this time.

Note➡ Determining importance in text is also related to main idea and summarizing.

Student's Name:_____   Date:_____

 # Determining Importance in Text: Written Assessment

Directions: Answer some questions about what you think about while you read.
Use the space below each question to write your answer.

A. Are there some parts of this text that are more important than the others? Which ones?
Why do you think they are the most important?

_____

_____

_____

B. What do you think the author thinks is most important so far in this text? What signals or
clues did the author use to make you think that was important?

_____

_____

_____

C. Choose one of the questions below to answer:

• You have just written about ideas, themes, words, pictures, and other parts of the text.
How does thinking about the more important parts help you to understand the text
better?

• Do you think or do anything while you are reading that helps you remember the
important parts?

• Do you ever have trouble remembering what is important after you read? How do you
solve that problem?

_____

_____

Student's Name:_____ Date:_____

 # Determining Importance in Text: Rubric

Directions:

Use this rubric to record the student's scores on each set of questions. Circle the number corresponding to the statement that best reflects the student's response. Consider all three questions when scoring the student.

1	No response, random guessing, inaccurate attempt to identify important elements.
2	Identifies some elements (primarily pictures) as more important to text meaning; isn't sure why these elements are important to overall meaning.
3	Identifies words, characters, and/or events as more important to overall meaning and makes some attempt to explain reasoning in expository text; uses text features such as bold print and captions to identify importance; explains why the concepts are important.
4	Identifies at least one key concept, idea, or theme as important in overall text meaning and clearly explains why.
5	Identifies multiple ideas or themes; may attribute them to different points of view; discusses author's stance or purpose and its relation to key themes and ideas in the text.

Observation Notes:

_____

_____

_____

_____

Student's Name:_____   Date:_____

Setting a Purpose for Reading: Oral Assessment

Directions: Read the following instructions to the student.
Record the student's responses below each question/statement.

A.   **What will this text help you learn about?**

_____

_____

B.   **When would you read (or listen to) another text like this? What for?**

_____

_____

C.   **Why would you pick this text to read on your own?**

_____

_____

Student's Name:_____ Date:_____

Setting a Purpose for Reading: Written Assessment

Directions: Answer some questions about what you think about while you read. Use the space below each question to write your answer.

A.   What will this text help you learn about?

_____

_____

_____

B.   When would you read another text like this? What for?

_____

_____

_____

C.   Why would you pick this text to read on your own?

_____

_____

_____

Student's Name:_____ Date:_____

 # Setting a Purpose for Reading: Rubric

Directions:

Use this rubric to record the student's scores on each set of questions. Circle the number corresponding to the statement that best reflects the student's response. Consider all three questions when scoring the student.

1	No response/irrelevant answers.
2	Attempts to identify reasons to read the text; thinking may be disconnected.
3	Thinking is tied to questions and text content.
4	Sets a reasonable purpose for reading and answers questions.
5	Can easily state the purpose for reading and talks about how readers set purposes for any/all texts.

Observation Notes:

_____

_____

_____

_____

Student's Name:_____ Date:_____

 # Monitoring Comprehension: Oral Assessment

Directions: Read the following instructions to the student. Record the student's responses below each question/statement.

A. What problems did you have while you (or I) were reading this text? Did you have more difficulty reading the words or understanding the ideas? When you are reading at other times, what kinds of problems do you usually have?

_____

_____

B. What did you do to solve any problems you had? How do you usually solve the problems you have when you read?

_____

_____

C. How do you know when you understand a text? What would you tell another student to try if he or she has trouble understanding?

_____

_____

D. Choose one of the questions below to ask the student:
   • We have just talked about the problems you have while reading and the ways in which you solve them. What is important to know when you have a problem while you are reading and (restate student's response)?
   • What are the different choices you can make to try to solve that problem?
   • What would you tell another reader who might not realize when a text doesn't make sense?

_____

_____

Student's Name:_____ Date:_____

 # Monitoring Comprehension: Written Assessment

Directions: Answer some questions about what you think about while you read. Use the space below each question to write your answer.

A.   What problems did you have while you were reading this text? Did you have more difficulty reading the words or understanding ideas? When you are reading at other times, what kinds of problems do you usually have?

_____

_____

_____

B.   What did you do to solve any problems you had? How do you usually solve the problems you have when you read?

_____

_____

_____

C.   How do you know that you completely understand a text? What would you tell another student to try if he or she is having trouble understanding?

_____

_____

_____

D.   Choose one of the questions below to answer:

• What is important to know when you are reading and have a problem?

• You have just written about problems you have during reading and the ways in which you solve them. What are the different choices you can make to try to solve those problems?

_____

Student's Name:_____ Date:_____

 # Monitoring Comprehension: Rubric

Use this rubric to record the student's scores on each set of questions. Circle the number corresponding to the statement that best reflects the student's response. Consider all three questions when scoring the student.

1	Little or no conscious awareness of reading process.
2	Identifies difficulties—problems are often at word level; little or no sense of the need to solve the problem; does not articulate strengths; identifies need to concentrate, talks about word-level solutions (i.e. sounding it out) for text-level comprehension problems.
3	Identifies problems at word, sentence, or schema level; can articulate and use a strategy to solve problems, usually at the word or sentence level.
4	Articulates and uses more than one strategy for solving problems; focuses on problems at the whole-text level.
5	Identifies problems at all levels; uses a variety of word level and comprehension strategies flexibly and appropriately given the context and the problem.

Observation Notes:

_____

_____

_____

_____

Visualizing (Using Sensory and Emotional Images): Oral Assessment

Directions: Read the following instructions to the student. Record the student's responses below each question/statement.

A. When you (or I) read the text, did you create pictures or images in your mind? Tell me everything you can about the images in your mind during the reading. What details in your images are not in the words (or pictures) in the book?

_____

_____

B. Can you remember creating pictures or images in your mind to help you understand the ideas when you read another book? Tell me everything you can about those pictures or images.

_____

_____

C. Choose one of the questions below to ask the students:

- We have just talked about the pictures or images you created in your mind while I read. Do those pictures or images help you to understand the text better?

- How do images help you understand more about what you read?

- What would you tell another reader about how to create images to better understand a text?

_____

_____

Student's Name:_____ Date:_____

 # Visualizing (Using Sensory and Emotional Images): Written Assessment

Directions: Answer some questions about what you think about while you read. Use the space below each question to write your answer.

A. When you were reading the text, did you create pictures or images in your mind? Tell everything you can about the images in your mind while you were just reading. What details in your image are not in the words or pictures in the book?

_____

_____

_____

B. Can you remember creating pictures or images in your mind to help you understand the ideas when you read another book? Tell everything you can about those pictures or images.

_____

_____

_____

C. Choose one of the questions below to answer:

• You have just written about the images you make in your mind while you read. Do those images help you to understand the text better?

• How do images help you understand more about what you read?

• What would you tell another reader about how to create images to better understand a text?

_____

_____

_____

Student's Name:_____ Date:_____

 # Visualizing (Using Sensory and Emotional Images): Rubric

Directions:

Use this rubric to record the student's scores on each set of questions. Circle the number corresponding to the statement that best reflects the student's response. Consider all three questions when scoring the student.

1	No response or unsure what he/she is supposed to describe.
2	Describes some visual or other sensory and/or emotional images; may be tied directly to text or a description of the picture in the text.
3	Describes own mental images, usually visual; images are somewhat elaborated from the literal text or existing picture and help him/her to understand more than he/she would have without creating the images. May include some emotional images that enhance the meaning.
4	Creates and describes multisensory and/or emotional images that extend and enrich the text; describes ways in which images help him/her to understand more about the text than would have been possible without the images.
5	Elaborates multisensory and emotional images to enhance comprehension; can articulate how the process enhances comprehension.

Observation Notes:

_____

_____

_____

_____

Student's Name:_____ Date:_____

 # Synthesizing and Retelling: Oral Assessment

Directions: Read the following instructions to the student. Record the student's responses below each question/statement.

    A.   If you were to tell another person about the text you (or I) just read and you could only use a few sentences, what would you say?

        _____

        _____

    B.   When you were reading (or listening to me read), did you change your mind about what the text is about? Can you show or tell me where you changed your mind and why?

        _____

        _____

    C.   Think about what you have just said about the story. What do you understand now that you didn't understand before? What do you think the author wants us to understand about this text? What opinions and ideas did you form about this text during and after reading it?

        _____

        _____

Note ➡ This assessment can also be used for "Retelling" (see Rubric on page 79) Summarizing is also related to synthesizing and retelling..

Synthesizing and Retelling: Written Assessment

Directions: Answer some questions about what you think about while you read.
Use the space below each question to write your answer.

A.   If you were to tell another person about the text you just read and you could only use a few sentences, what would you say?

   _____

   _____

   _____

B.   When you were reading, did you change your mind about what the text is about? Describe the place in the story where you changed your mind. Why did you change your mind?

   _____

   _____

   _____

C.   Think about what you have just written about the story. What do you understand now that you didn't understand before? What do you think the author wants us to understand about this text? What opinions and ideas did you form about this text during and after reading it?

   _____

   _____

   _____

Student's Name:_____ Date:_____

 # Synthesizing: Rubric

Directions:

Use this rubric to record the student's scores on each set of questions. Circle the number corresponding to the statement that best reflects the student's response. Consider all three questions when scoring the student.

1	Random or no response; may give title.
2	Identifies some text events—random or illogical order.
3	Synthesizes with some awareness of event sequence—beginning, middle, end, or the chronology of the text as it has been read so far. Understands that the sequence appears to aid comprehension; may talk about how he/she changed his/her mind about overall story meaning during reading.
4	Enhances meaning in text with synthesis; may incorporate own schema; uses story elements or structures to enhance the synthesis; may identify key themes; describes how thinking evolved from the beginning to the end of the passage.
5	Succinct synthesis using internalized story/genre/text structure; identifies key themes; may articulate how synthesizing promotes deeper comprehension—can articulate how flexibility in thinking throughout the piece promotes comprehension, talks about feelings the piece evoked.

Observation Notes:

_____

_____

_____

_____

Student's Name:_____ Date:_____

 # Retelling: Rubric

Directions:

Use this rubric to record the student's scores on each set of questions. Circle the number corresponding to the statement that best reflects the student's response. Consider all three questions when scoring the student.

1	Random response; may be related to text; may give title.
2	Retelling reveals beginning awareness of event sequence.
3	Uses story elements/genre structure to organize a relatively accurate summary or retelling of story's beginning, middle, and end.
4	Story elements/genre structure are clear in an accurate summary or retelling; refers to interactions between story elements (how problem affects character, how setting changes problem, etc.).
5	Uses all story elements/genre structure and inferences to capture key themes in the text; points out relationships between elements; talks about how the overall meaning is influenced.

Observation Notes:

_____

_____

_____

_____

Student's Name:_____ Date:_____

Text Structure/Structural Patterns: Oral Assessment

Directions: Read the following instructions to the student. Record the student's responses below each question/statement.

There are some parts of the texts you read that you find in every text. These are called text elements or structures. For example, there are usually characters, a problem, and events in a fiction story. I want to ask about text elements now.

A. **In this text, did you find text elements or structures? What were they?**

_____

_____

B. **How were text elements or structures in this text used?**

_____

_____

C. **How did those text elements or structures help you better understand the text?**

_____

_____

D. **How can text elements or structures help you better understand any text you read?**

_____

_____

Student's Name:_____ Date:_____

 # Text Structure/Structural Patterns: Written Assessment

Directions: Answer some questions about what you think about while you read. Use the space below each question to write your answer.

There are some parts of the texts you read that you find in every text. These are called text elements or structures. For example, there are usually characters, a problem, and events in a fiction story. Write about text elements now.

A. In this text, what elements or structures did you notice?

_____

_____

_____

B. What signals or clues does an author use to show the reader what elements or structures are used?

_____

_____

_____

C. How did the text elements or structures help you better understand the text?

_____

_____

_____

D. How can text elements or structures help you better understand any text you read?

_____

_____

_____

Student's Name:_____ Date:_____

 # Text Structure/Structural Patterns: Rubric

Directions:

Use this rubric to record the student's scores on each set of questions. Circle the number corresponding to the statement that best reflects the student's response. Consider all three questions when scoring the student.

1	No response; restates what examiner says.
2	Lists one or more elements/structures not named by examiner (i.e., character, setting, bold text, charts, graphs, etc.).
3	Points out where/how the author introduced a text element.
4	Describes how elements/structures in text are central to meaning.
5	Discusses ways in which text elements/structures focus a reader's attention, permitting the reader to recall important information and/or make inferences.

Observation Notes:

_____

_____

_____

_____

Works Cited

Block, C., Gambrell, L.,& Pressley, M. (2002). Improving Comprehension Instruction: An Urgent Priority. In *Improving Comprehension Instruction* (pp. 3–6). San Francisco: Jossey-Bass.

Burns, P., Roe, B., & Ross, E. (1999). *Teaching Reading in Today's Elementary Schools.* Boston: Houghton Mifflin Company.

Cunningham, P., & Allington R. (2003). *Classrooms That Work: They Can All Read and Write.* Boston: Allyn and Bacon.

Duke N., & Pearson, D. (2002). Effective Practices for Developing Reading Comprehension. In *What Research Has to Say About Reading Instruction* (pp. 205–242). Newark, DE: International Reading Association.

Harvey, S., & Goudvis, A. (2000). *Strategies That Work: Teaching Comprehension to Enhance Learning.* York, ME: Stenhouse.

Honig, B., Diamond, L., Gutlohn, L., & Mahler, J. (2000). *Teaching Reading Sourcebook for Kindergarten Through Eighth Grade.* Novato: Arena Press.

Keene, E., & Zimmermann, S. (1997). *Mosaic of Thought.* Portsmouth, NH: Heinemann.

Pearson, P. D., Roehler, L., Dole, J., & Duffy, G. (1992). Developing Expertise in Reading Comprehension. In S. J. Samuels & A. E. Farstrup (Eds.), *What Research Has to Say About Reading Instruction* (2nd ed., pp. 145–199). Newark, DE: International Reading Association.

Product Suggestions and Recommended Reading

Page eight of this book offers ideas about what instructional materials to use after you conduct the assessments in this book. There are many products that can provide reading comprehension instruction. You may wish to consider one or more of the following products:

Teacher Created Materials Products

- *Exploring Nonfiction: Reading in the Content Areas*, kit levels K–Secondary
- *Nonfiction Reading and Writing for Summer School, After School, and Other Special Programs*, levels K–5
- *Reading in the Content Areas: Exploring Nonfiction Supplement*, levels 2–5

To find these products, visit *http://www.tcmpub.com* or call 1-800-858-7339.

Shell EducationPublishing Products

- *Successful Strategies for Reading in the Content Areas*, strategies for grades 1–2, 3–5, 6–8
- *Teaching Reading in the Content Areas*, a professional book

To find these products, visit *http://www.shelleducation.com* or call 1-877-777-3450.

Beach City Press Products

- *Practice with Purpose: Standards-Based Comprehension Strategies & Skills*, levels 1–Secondary
- *Reading Comprehension: Developing Fiction and Nonfiction Skills*, levels 1–8

To find these products, visit *http://www.beachcitypress.com* or call 1-888-227-3539.

Recommended Reading

Additionally, the book *Mosaic of Thought*, co-authored by Ellin Keene, has many reading comprehension instruction ideas. This author also wrote the forewords to *Reading with Meaning* by Debbie Miller and *I Read It, But I Don't Get It* by Cris Tovani. She recommends these professional books for their ideas about reading comprehension as well. She also recommends *Strategies That Work* by Stephanie Harvey and Anne Goudvis.

Notes

Notes

Notes

Notes